How to Teach British Literature

Student Review Questions and Tests

Elizabeth McCallum Marlow

WESTBOW
PRESS®
A DIVISION OF THOMAS NELSON
& ZONDERVAN

WestBow Press books may be ordered through booksellers or by contacting:

WestBow Press
A Division of Thomas Nelson & Zondervan
1663 Liberty Drive
Bloomington, IN 47403
www.westbowpress.com
1 (866) 928-1240

ISBN: 978-1-9736-1393-0 (sc)
ISBN: 978-1-9736-1392-3 (e)

Print information available on the last page.

WestBow Press rev. date: 02/12/2018

To the Teacher

The following review questions and tests are designed to be used in conjunction with *How to Teach British Literature: A Practical Teaching Guide*. All review questions and tests are included in the teaching guide and reproduced in this booklet with answers omitted.

Review questions

Copy and distribute a set of review questions to your class. Students break into small groups and refer to their literature books and notes as each group discusses the questions. Every student answers the questions in his or her notebook. On an assigned day, students hand in their notebooks with the completed questions for grading. At a later date, the teacher should review with the class appropriate answers to each set of review questions. The teacher may choose to use some of the questions on tests and semester exams.

Tests

Test procedure[1]

A. Taking tests[2]

Have students clear their desks and take out a pen. Distribute tests. Require students to place a cover sheet on top of their tests and move it down to cover answers as they take the test. The teacher may also wish to arrange students' desks at some distance apart. Instruct students to use the back of the test if they require more space for their responses. As students finish a test, they should place it face down on their desks and work on other assignments until everyone has completed the test. Collect the tests.

B. Reviewing tests

Distribute graded tests and review answers. While grading the tests, the teacher may opt to note down excellent responses and ask individual students to read those responses to the class. Take time to answer students' questions about both questions and responses.

---

[1]   I have found the following procedures to be effective. Other teachers may prefer to adopt methods that are more suited to the needs of a particular class.

[2]   Some tests require the teacher to copy certain excerpts or poems and attach them to the back of the test.

Literature holds up a mirror to life and in so doing allows us to better understand ourselves and others.

Contents

Review questions on *Beowulf*

Name _____

1. Provide a one-sentence thematic statement for this epic.

2. Identify the setting or settings of the excerpts we read.

3. Name and define several poetic devices found in Anglo-Saxon poetry.

4. Identify these people: Hygelac, Hrothgar, Ecgtheow's son, son of Weohstan.

5. Define these three items: Wyrd, beot, didactic aside.

6. What important contrast does the *Beowulf* poet establish in his opening lines?

7. Explain the comitatus.

8. What are J. R. R. Tolkien's connections to the epic?

9. Give several examples of the way the *Beowulf* poet combines pagan ideas with Christian beliefs.

10. List several differences between the so-called two halves of the epic, Beowulf's battles with the monsters versus his battle with the dragon.

11. What is your opinion of Wiglaf? Support your comments with reference to the poem.

12. How does Beowulf exemplify an epic hero?

Review questions on *The Canterbury Tales*

Name _____

1. When Chaucer describes the pilgrims in his Prologue, he includes details of external appearance that suggest the personality of a pilgrim. Describe two or three pilgrims in terms of this medieval belief in physiognomy.

2. Taken as a group, what do Chaucer's pilgrims represent? Summarize the circumstances of their pilgrimage.

3. How do we know that the Knight is "a perfect gentle knight"?

4. List two or three other exemplary pilgrims.

5. What is meant by the two voices that operate throughout the Prologue?

6. List two or more examples of portraits in which the two voices are particularly evident.

7. Explain how the portrait of the Prioress is a satire of the medieval church.

8. Explain the ambiguity of Madame Eglantyne's brooch.

9. Explain the irony of the Monk's portrait.

10. Summarize details Chaucer gives us about the Wife of Bath prior to her going on the pilgrimage to Canterbury. Why is she going on this journey?

11. Summarize the three ways in which the old hag in "The Wife of Bath's Tale" refutes the knight's three objections to marrying her.

12. Briefly explain how "The Pardoner's Tale" ironically fits the personality of the Pardoner.

13. Briefly explain how the irony in "The Nun's Priest's Tale" targets Madame Eglantyne.

14. Chaucer has been accused of being a misogynist. With reference to the Prologue and one of the Tales we read, support this opinion.

15. Think about the genres of the three tales we read. List each tale and give its genre.

16. Based on what criteria does the Host suggest the pilgrims select a winning tale?

Review questions on Renaissance poetry

Name _____

Support your responses with close reference to the poems.

1. Briefly summarize the autobiographical background of Wyatt's sonnet "Whoso List to Hunt."

2. Discuss the effectiveness of Wyatt's metaphor in this poem.

3. Name the poetic device with which Sidney opens his sonnet 31 and list in modern English several questions he addresses to the moon.

4. What is the theme of Shakespeare's sonnet 73?

5. Explain how Shakespeare's imagery contributes to the theme of sonnet 73.

6. Why is Shakespeare's sonnet 130 anti-Petrarchan?

7. Provide adjectives that define the moods of the speaker in Shakespeare's sonnet 29.

8. Summarize the content of sonnet 29.

9. Summarize the situation Spenser explores in sonnet 75.

10. State the universal theme this sonnet conveys.

11. Identify the different tones of Marlowe's pastoral "The Passionate Shepherd" and Raleigh's reply to Marlowe's poem.

12. Identify the metaphysical conceit in Donne's reply to Marlowe's pastoral.

13. Explain why C. Day Lewis's reply to Marlowe's pastoral is highly cynical.

14. <u>Turn in your questions</u> then write out the Shakespearean sonnet you have memorized.

Review questions on *Macbeth* Acts I–III

Name _____

Support your answers with close reference to the play.

1. Identify Shakespeare's source for *Macbeth*.

2. What is the setting of the play and what is Shakespeare's predominant meter throughout the play?

3. Explain the difference between Banquo and Macbeth's initial reactions to the witches.

4. How do we know that Duncan is a poor judge of character?

5. What is Macbeth's tragic flaw?

6. How does Lady Macbeth induce her husband to murder the king?

7. Explain how Lady Macbeth manipulates events before and immediately after Duncan's murder.

8. After Macbeth and Banquo meet the witches, Macbeth appears to be deep in thought and momentarily unaware of Banquo's presence. Read these lines and explain the significance of Macbeth's reply:

Banquo: Worthy Macbeth, we stay upon your leisure [we await your convenience].

Macbeth: Give me your favor. My dull brain was wrought

With things forgotten.

9. How do Donalbain and Malcolm react to their father's murder? What action do they take?

10. Read Macbeth's words that end Act I and explain the significance of the last line:

I am settled, and bend up

Each corporal agent to this terrible feat.

Away, and mock the time [mislead the world] with fairest show:

False face must hide what the false heart doth know.

11. Identify two functions of the Porter's scene.

12. Banquo is highly respected throughout Scotland. Explain how Macbeth persuades the hired assassins to murder this noble thane.

13. After Macbeth has murdered Duncan, he tells his wife, "We have scotched [wounded] the snake not killed it." Explain his comment.

14. Why does Shakespeare allow Fleance to escape when his father is murdered?

15. What effect does Banquo's ghost have on Macbeth during the banquet scene?

16. What action does Lady Macbeth take when her husband has "displaced the mirth" of the banquet?

Review questions on *Macbeth* Acts IV–V

Name _____

Support your answers with close reference to the play.

1. At the beginning of Act IV when Macbeth returns to the witches, they show him four apparitions. Explain how two of the apparitions give him a false sense of security.

2. What is the significance of the mirror held by the last apparition?

3. Why does Shakespeare include a lengthy conversation between Lady Macduff and her son before they are both murdered?

4. Explain whether Shakespeare adheres to or violates the principle of decorum when Lady Macduff and her son are murdered.

5. If Macbeth were a murderous villain, the events of the play would not be tragic. Give two reasons why one has to acknowledge that Macbeth is indeed a tragic hero.

6. During Act V, two thanes talk together. Explain this comment made by Angus:
   Now does he feel his title
   Hang lose about him, like a giant's robe
   Upon a dwarfish thief.

7. In your opinion, what is the play's climax? Explain.

8. Explain why the following lines are so poignant:

> My way of life
> Is fall'n into the sear [withered], the yellow leaf,
> And that which should accompany old age,
> As honor, love, obedience, troops of friends,
> I must not look to have.

9. In your own words, briefly summarize the main idea conveyed in this memorable passage:

> Out, out, brief candle!
> Life's but a walking shadow, a poor player
> That struts and frets his hour upon the stage
> And then is heard no more. It is a tale
> Told by an idiot, full of sound and fury,
> Signifying nothing.

10. Give two reasons or more why this play is, in part, a compliment to Shakespeare's patron, King James I.

11. One device Shakespeare uses is the foil character. Explain how one character is a foil for Macbeth.

12. The atmosphere of the play contributes significantly to its meaning. Identify the dominant mood.

13. Write out a one-sentence theme for this tragedy.

Review questions on 17th century poetry

Name _____

1. Explain why the Sons of Ben were named "Cavalier Poets."

2. What differences in style and content did you notice between cavalier and metaphysical poetry?

3. What is the dominant tone of Suckling's poetry? What appears to be his attitude to love?

4. List some significant biographical facts about both John Donne and George Herbert.

5. Referring to pertinent stanzas, briefly explain the central metaphysical conceit in Donne's "Valediction Forbidding Mourning."

6. Dr. Johnson had a decidedly mediocre opinion of the metaphysical poets. In your own words, explain why he apparently disliked this type of poetry.

7. List several differences in the poetry of Donne and Herbert.

8. Provide an adjective that describes the tone of Donne's Holy Sonnet 10.

9. Identify the paradox in Holy Sonnet 10.

10. List the ways in which Herbert's four stanzas are connected in "Virtue." Explain how the fourth stanza contrasts with the first three.

11. Herbert's "The Altar" is an emblematic poem. How does this fact enhance its meaning?

12. Define these four items then explain their relevance to Marvell's poem "To His Coy Mistress": *carpe diem*, syllogism, allusion, hyperbole.

13–17: Identify the author and make some significant comments about the following lines:

13. Gather ye rosebuds while ye may,
    Old time is still a-flying.

14. Stone walls do not a prison make,
    Nor iron bars a cage.

15. Out upon it, I have loved
    Three whole days together.

16. But at my back I always hear
    Time's wingèd chariot hurrying near.

17. Farewell, thou child of my right hand and joy.
    My sin was too much hope of thee…

18. What conflict arises between Satan and Beelzebub in the excerpt we read from *Paradise Lost*?

19. State Milton's theme in *Paradise Lost*.

20. How does Milton suggest Satan's size?

21. What does Satan mean when he asserts, "The mind is its own place, and in itself / Can make a Heaven of Hell, a Hell of Heaven"?

22. In the eighteenth century, William Blake declared that Milton, at least subconsciously, admired Satan. Explain your opinion of Blake's assertion.

Review questions on Restoration and 18th century literature

Name _____

1–10: Identify the author and title and write a significant comment on the following quotations:

1. The shepherd in Virgil grew at last acquainted with love and found him a native of the rocks.

2. True wit is Nature to advantage dress'd,
   What oft was thought, but ne'er so well expressed.

3. Commonly a wretch who supports with insolence and is paid with flattery.

4. About four o'clock in the morning, my Lady Batten sent me a cart to carry away all my money, and plate, and best things, to Sir W. Rider's at Bednall Green.

5. Sharp violins proclaim
   Their jealous pangs and desperation,
   Fury, frantic indignation….

6. I hope it is no very cynical asperity not to confess obligation where no benefit has been received.

7. Nay…if you will venture upon that score, name of God go in; for, depend upon it, it will be a sermon to you…'Tis a speaking sight…

8. True ease in writing comes from art not chance
    As those move easiest who have learned to dance.

9. …but, Lord! to consider the madness of the people of the town who will (because they are forbid) come in crowds…to see them buried; but we agreed on some orders for the prevention thereof.

10. A harmless drudge.

11. Identify three differences in the accounts of Pepys and Defoe when describing the Fire of London.

Review questions on Romantic poetry

Name _____

Support your answers with close reference to the poems.

1. In what important ways is Romantic poetry a reaction to the neoclassic literature of the previous age?

2. Why do scholars date the beginning of the Romantic era at 1798?

3. Refer to the final three stanzas of Wordsworth's poem entitled "The Tables Turned." How do these stanzas reflect a major sentiment of the Romantic era?

4. Reread Wordsworth's lines that begin "My heart leaps up when I behold / A rainbow in the sky." Explain the difference between Wordsworth's reaction and a Christian's reaction to a rainbow.

5. Refer to Wordsworth's sonnet "Composed upon Westminster Bridge." How does the poet's use of personification add to the beauty of the scene before him?

6. Refer to the sonnet that begins "It is a beauteous evening, calm and free." Explain how the structure is ideally suited to the content of the poem. What Romantic idea does the poem convey?

7. Defend this statement about "The Ancient Mariner": Coleridge's poem could be read as an exploration of sin, punishment, repentance, and forgiveness.

8 – 12: Identify the poet who wrote the following lines and make some significant observations about the lines. For example, you could discuss the way they reflect Romantic tendencies, you could comment on pertinent poetic devices, or you could discuss anything else you know about the poems.

8. The lone and level sands stretch far away.

9. England hath need of thee: she is a fen
    Of stagnant waters: altar, sword, and pen,
    Fireside, the heroic wealth of hall and bower,
    Have forfeited their ancient English dower
    Of inward happiness

10. Then felt I like some watcher of the skies
    When a new planet swims into his ken;
    Or like stout Cortez when with eagle eyes
    He stares at the Pacific...

11. The smiles that win, the tints that glow,
    But tell of days in goodness spent.

12. Then in a wailful choir the small gnats mourn
    Along the river sallows, born aloft
    Or sinking as the light wind lives or dies.

13. Identify the theme of Shelley's "Ozymandias." Explain the irony operating throughout the poem.

Review questions on *Pride and Prejudice*

Name _____

1. What is the significance of the entail?

2. Explain the irony of Austen's opening sentence: "It is a truth universally acknowledged that a young man in possession of a good fortune must be in want of a wife."

3. Who lives at the following places: Rosings Park, Pemberley, Netherfield Park, and Longbourn?

4. What is the function of the village of Meryton in this novel?

5. Is Elizabeth Bennet a dynamic or a static character? Explain.

6. What is your opinion of Mr. Bennet as a husband and father? Explain.

7. Summarize Elizabeth's first and later impressions of Wickham.

8. What is your opinion of Lydia Bennet?

9. What is Mary Bennet's principal character trait?

10 – 21: Identify the characters these comments pertain to and explain the context and the significance of each passage:

10. "Can he be a sensible man?"

11. He really believed, that were it not for the inferiority of her connections, he should be in some danger.

12. "Heaven forbid! —*That* would be the greatest misfortune of all! —To find a man agreeable whom one is determined to hate!"

13. "_____, to be sure, was neither sensible nor agreeable; his society was irksome, and his attachment to her must be imaginary."

14. "They are all for what they can get. I am sorry to say it of them, but so it is. It makes me very nervous and poorly, to be thwarted so in my own family, and to have neighbors who think of themselves before anybody else."

15. "Yes, Miss Elizabeth, you will have the honor of seeing _____ on the ensuing Sunday at church, and I need not say you will be delighted with her. She is all affability and condescension, and I doubt not but you will be honored with some portion of her notice when service is over."

16. "If you ——— will not take the trouble of checking her exuberant spirits, and of teaching her that her present pursuits are not to be the business of her life, she will soon be beyond the reach of amendment."

17. "In vain have I struggled. It will not do. My feelings will not be repressed. You must allow me to tell you…"

18. "He is the best landlord, and the best master…that ever lived."

19. She was a woman of mean understanding, little information, and uncertain temper. When she was discontented, she fancied herself nervous.

20. "vanity, not love, has been my folly…I have courted prepossession and ignorance, and driven reason away, where either were concerned. Till this moment I never knew myself."

21. "I am seriously displeased."

Review questions on Victorian Poetry

Name _____

1. Define what two types of adventure Tennyson's Ulysses wishes to pursue.

2. Why did Tennyson write *In Memoriam* and what genre of poem is it?

3. What is the meaning of Browning's title "Prospice"? Why is it an appropriate title for the poem?

4. Explain the difference between Browning and Tennyson's attitudes to death conveyed in "Prospice" and "Crossing the Bar."

5. Identify the author and structure of "Up-Hill." Why is the title effective?

6. Briefly define the Duke of Ferrara's personality as it is conveyed in "My Last Duchess." Explain the poem's central irony.

7. What is the controlling metaphor in "Dover Beach," and what does that metaphor represent?

8. Although "Dover Beach" was written when the poet was on his honeymoon, it is inaccurate to call it a romantic poem. Explain this paradox.

9. Provide an adjective that describes the mood of "The Darkling Thrush." Explain the function of the thrush in Hardy's poem. What is the speaker's response to the thrush's song?

10. How does Browning convey a highly romantic mood in "Meeting at Night"?

11. What is the theme of "To an Athlete Dying Young"? How is that theme conveyed?

12. What is the speaker's main concern in "The Man He Killed"? How is the concern conveyed?

13. What is the theme of "The Man He Killed"?

14. What is the central irony of "The Convergence of the Twain"?

15. Briefly comment on Hardy's attitude to the *Titanic*'s tragic fate.

Review questions on *Tess of the d'Urbervilles*

Name _____

1. Mention several circumstances of Tess's life that support Hardy's fatalism.

2. What is the name of Tess's baby and why does Tess bury it in a neglected part of the church graveyard?

3. After the baby's death, where does Tess find work and what kind of work does she do?

4. Provide the names of two girls who work where Tess gets a job after her baby's death.

5. Explain Hardy's fatalism in this passage:
   He was the pedestrian…the passing stranger who had come she knew not whence, had danced with others but not with her, had slightingly left, and gone on his way with his friends.

6. When Tess writes to tell her mother that she is going to marry Angel, her mother writes back. What advice does her mother give her? What is your opinion of this advice?

7. On her wedding day, Tess writes Angel a note explaining her "Bygone Trouble." Why doesn't Angel read the note?

8. What fact emerges about Angel Clare that makes us realize he is a hypocrite?

9. After Angel walks in his sleep and places Tess in a coffin against a wall in some abbey ruins, she guides him back to the house where they are staying. Explain what is implied in this passage:

   Thus she conducted him by the arm to the stone bridge in front of their residence… Tess's feet were quite bare, and the stones hurt her and chilled her to the bone; but Clare was in his woolen stockings and appeared to feel no discomfort.

10. The other girls at the diary are in love with Angel Clare. How does one of them respond when Angel suggests that she accompany him to Brazil?

11. After Angel abandons Tess, she finds it difficult to get work. Where does she eventually find employment and what kind of work does she do?

12. Who convinces Angel that he was wrong to abandon Tess?

13. What event causes Tess to return home to her family?

14. Alec relentlessly pursues Tess, and she repeatedly rejects him. How does he finally persuade her to give in to him?

15. What lie does Alec tell Tess concerning Angel?

16. Why do you think Hardy chose to relate Alec's murder from the perspective of the landlady at the lodging house in Sandbourne rather than from Tess's viewpoint? Does Hardy adhere to the principle of decorum here?

17. Where do Angel and Tess briefly rest before she is arrested? Why is this location significant?

18. In the final paragraph, Hardy quotes the Greek dramatist Aeschylus: "the President of the Immortals…had ended his sport with Tess." Explain Hardy's allusion.

Review questions on *Jane Eyre*

Name _____

1–2: Explain the irony in these passages:

1. He gorged himself habitually at table, which made him bilious and gave him a dim and bleared eye and flabby cheeks. He ought now to have been at school; but his mamma had taken him home for a month or two "on account of his delicate health." Mr. Miles, the master, affirmed that he would do very well if he had fewer cakes and sweetmeats sent him from home, but the mother's heart turned from an opinion so harsh and inclined rather to the more refined idea that ——'s sallowness was owing to over-application and, perhaps, to pining after home.

2. After Mr. Brocklehurst assures Mrs. Reed that "Humility is a Christian grace," his daughter offers this information:
"the girls at Lowood are quiet and plain…with their hair combed behind their ears… they are almost like poor people's children and they looked at my dress and mamma's as if they had never seen a silk gown before."

3. Jane is punished after John Reed's physical attack on her during which she likens him to "the Roman emperors." Why is her punishment so cruel?

4. Who suggests that Jane should be sent away to school?

5. Provide one or two adjectives that define the characters of these people:
Miss Temple:

Miss Scatcherd:

Mr. Brocklehurst:

Helen:

6. How does Helen counsel Jane?

7. What event occurs at Lowood School that creates public outcry at the appalling conditions there?

8. When Bessie visits Jane at Lowood, she asks whether Jane has heard from her father's relatives, the Eyres. Bessie tells Jane that a Mr. Eyre came to Gateshead to see Jane after she had been sent away to school. What literary device is Brontë using here?

9. Before she actually meets Edward Rochester, Jane gets a favorable impression of him when _____ tells her that he is highly respected and liked by his servants and tenants. (Fill in the blank.)

10. Describe Jane's first meeting with Rochester.

11. Why is Adèle Varens Rochester's ward?

12. How does Jane save Rochester's life while she lives at Thornfield?

13. Provide several adjectives that define Blanche Ingram's character.

14. A so-called gypsy arrives at Thornfield supposedly to tell the people's fortunes. Why does the gypsy wish to interview Jane?

15. Mrs. Reed has always hated Jane. At the end of her life, she regrets doing two things to hurt Jane. For one thing, she broke her promise to her husband to raise Jane as her own child. Apart from her obvious cruelty, what was the other thing she did to hurt Jane?

16. After Jane accepts Rochester's first proposal of marriage, what dramatic event occurs?

17. What does this event symbolize?

18. What deranged act does Rochester's mad wife perform after Jane and Rochester are engaged?

19. What does Bertha's act symbolize?

20. Who is Mr. Mason?

21. Who breaks off the marriage by announcing that Rochester already has a wife and what details of the previous marriage does he or she provide?

22. Why does Rochester marry Bertha Mason?

23. Briefly describe St. John Rivers.

24. Why doesn't St. John marry Rosamond Oliver, the woman he loves and who loves him?

25. When Jane discovers she is an heiress, what does she do with her money?

26. When St. John proposes marriage to Jane, what happens to prevent her from accepting his proposal?

27. What dramatic events occur at Thornfield before Jane's return?

28. Do you think Jane and Rochester will be happy together? Why or why not?

29. Is Rochester a dynamic or static character? Explain.

30. Explain why it is accurate to call Rochester a Byronic hero.

Review questions on *Great Expectations*

Name _____

1. This novel tells the story of a young man's education. Pip learns through suffering a great deal about himself and matures into a wiser man. Drawing on several incidents in the book, list several lessons he learns that strike you as important.

2. The scene in the graveyard has been widely admired as one of the best opening scenes of any novel. Why do you think it has received such high praise?

3. Two escaped convicts hide in the graveyard. How does Dickens elicit our sympathy for the one to whom Pip brings food and not the other?

4. Read these comments about Mrs. Joe and explain what they reveal about her:
    Mrs. Joe was a very clean housekeeper, but had an exquisite art of making her cleanliness more uncomfortable and unacceptable than dirt itself…My sister having so much to do was going to church vicariously.

5 – 13: Name the people described here:

5. A tough, high-shouldered, stooping old man of a sawdusty fragrance.

6. A little dry brown corrugated old woman with a small face that might have been made of walnut shells…

7. He was a broad shouldered, loose-limbed, swarthy fellow of great strength, never in a hurry, and always slouching.

8. She was not beautiful—she was common…but she was pleasant and wholesome and sweet-tempered.

9. I checked off again in detail his large head, his dark complexion, his deep-set eyes, his bushy black eyebrows, his large watch chain, his strong black dots of beard and whisker, and even the smell of scented soap on his great hand.

10. The pale young gentleman

11. A wild beast tamed

12. The Aged

13. The abhorrence in which I held the man, the dread I had of him, the repugnance with which I shrank from him, could not have been exceeded if he had been some terrible beast.

14. Explain how Jaggers is connected to four main characters.

15. How does Dickens use Jaggers as part of his criticism of the British legal system?

16. What is Herbert Pocket's main character flaw?

17. How do Herbert and Pip deal with their debts?

18. Why is Mrs. Joe's funeral a piece of social criticism?

19. Apart from Mrs. Joe's funeral, how else does Dickens satirize Victorian mores in this novel?

20. What ironies are involved in the identities of Estella's parents?

21. Joe is a man of integrity. Mention some ways by which Dickens conveys this idea.

22. What coincidence is involved in Pip's rescue from death at the hands of Orlick?

23. The novel explores the idea of atonement. Explain how this theme applies to Miss Havisham.

24. List aspects of the novel's fairy-tale quality.

25. Which of the three endings do you prefer: Dickens's first ending, his second published ending, the movie ending? Explain your preference.

Review questions on *Lord of the Flies*

Name _____

1. Identify the main character traits of Simon, Ralph, Piggy, and Jack.

2 - 6: Discuss the symbolism of the following items:
2. The conch shell

3. Piggy's specs

4. The mythical beast

5. The signal fire

6. The Lord of the Flies

7. In what way does the island on which the boys are stranded first seem to be Edenic?

8. What does the island become at the end of the novel? Why does this happen?

9. Who is the novel's antagonist?

10. When is the existence of a beast first introduced?

11. What is the first major event that symbolizes the breakdown of the boys' world?

12. Identify some reasons why the boys' society breaks down.

13. What is Golding's central idea that the novel graphically illustrates?

14. What are Jack's assignments while the boys remain on the island?

15. What vital fact does Simon realize that the other boys do not?

16. Why do the other boys kill Simon?

17. Explain why the novel's conclusion is a classic *deus ex machina* ending.

18. What is your opinion of the naval officer?

Review questions on *The Great Divorce*

Name _____

1 – 6: Name the pet sin that keeps the following characters from remaining in heaven:

1. The Ghost of an Episcopal bishop

2. The Big Ghost

3. The Ghost of Robert's wife

4. The painter Ghost

5. The well-dressed female Ghost

6. The Ghost of Michael's mother

7. Summarize some details that suggest the dreariness of Lewis's hell.

8. Summarize some details of Lewis's heaven that contrast with hell.

9. Why does Lewis describe the grass in heaven as solid and unbending?

10. Summarize what happens to the Ghost with the lizard on its shoulder.

11. Write a paragraph in which you state all you know about Sarah Smith.

12. Why is Lewis's choice of a dream vision for this novel so effective?

13. Explain the meaning of Lewis's title, *The Great Divorce*. Be sure to refer to William Blake.

Review questions on modern and contemporary poetry

Name _____

Quote from or paraphrase the poetry whenever possible.

1. Identify the tone of Rupert Brooke's poem "The Old Vicarage, Grantchester."

2. Rupert Brooke's "The Soldier" was written while the poet was fighting in World War I. The emotion it expresses is similar to another poem we studied that has nothing to do with war. Name that poem and its author.

3. What main concern is conveyed in Siegfried Sassoon's poem "Base Details"?

4. Like Siegfried Sassoon, Wilfred Owen wrote poetry that conveyed his hatred of war. What metaphorical image runs through his anti-war poem entitled "Anthem for Doomed Youth"?

5. List several contrasts Owen makes in the two halves of the sonnet "Anthem for Doomed Youth."

6. Explain how we know that "Journey of the Magi" is an exploration of Eliot's conversion experience.

7. List some of Eliot's allusions to Christ in this poem.

8. Identify and explain the two allusions in the headnote of "The Hollow Men."

9. Whom is Yeats addressing in the poem that begins, "When you are old and gray and full of sleep"? What does the poet want the addressee to do?

10. What is the predominant tone of "The Lake Isle of Innisfree"? Explain the reference to Innisfree.

11. Identify the two speakers in Henry Reed's "Naming of Parts."

12. What is Reed satirizing in "Naming of Parts"?

13. "The Unknown Citizen" is another satiric poem. What is W. H. Auden satirizing?

14. Identify three of the four men to whom Dylan Thomas refers in "Do Not Go Gentle into That Good Night." What do these men have in common?

15. In what one essential way does the poet's father differ from all these men?

16. Summarize the personality traits of Ted Hughes's hawk in "Hawk Roosting."

17. Explain the multiple meanings of Seamus Heaney's title "Digging."

18. As he watches his father digging a flowerbed, does the poet regret his own lack of physical digging? Explain.

19. "Church Going" is another title that conveys several meanings. Explain.

20. Summarize the personality of the cyclist in "Church Going."

21. What is your personal reaction to "Church Going"?

22. What is J. Alfred Prufrock's main problem?

23 - 28: Briefly explain the significance of the following lines from "The Love Song of J. Alfred Prufrock":

23. In the room the women come and go
    Talking of Michelangelo.

24. There will be time, there will be time
    To prepare a face to meet the faces that you meet.

25. They will say: "How his hair is growing thin!"

26. I should have been a pair of ragged claws
    Scuttling across the floors of silent seas.

27. No! I am not Prince Hamlet, nor was meant to be;
Am an attendant lord, one that will do
To swell the progress, start a scene or two,
Advise the prince, no doubt, an easy tool,
Deferential, glad to be of use,
Politic, cautious, and meticulous;
Full of high sentence, but a bit obtuse;
At times, indeed, almost ridiculous—
Almost, at times, the Fool.

28. I do not think they will sing for me.

Macbeth Acts I-III Test

Name_____

1. What is the significance of Macbeth's first words: "So foul and fair a day I have not seen"?

2. Why is soliloquy in Shakespeare's plays (or any other play) so important?

3. After Macbeth and Banquo meet the witches, Macbeth appears to be deep in thought and temporarily unaware of Banquo's presence. Read these lines:

    Banquo: Worthy Macbeth, we stay [wait] upon your leisure.

    Macbeth: Give me your favor. My dull brain was wrought

               With things forgotten.

    Explain the significance of Macbeth's reply.

4. How does Shakespeare establish in our minds Macbeth's heroic status early in the play?

5. Based on the first three Acts, summarize what you know about Lady Macbeth's character.

6. What is effective about the letter technique that Shakespeare adopts in Act I?

7. What are the two main reasons why Macbeth decides to kill Duncan?

8. Name the reasons why Macbeth is reluctant to murder Duncan.

9. Give one valid reason for Macbeth's hallucinating about a dagger.

10. Name two reasons for the Porter's scene.

11. Sometime after Macbeth has murdered Duncan, we hear his thoughts in a soliloquy:
    To be thus is nothing, but to be safely thus—
    Our fears in Banquo stick deep,
    And in his royalty of nature reigns that
    Which would be feared…
    For Banquo's issue have I filed [defiled] my mind;
    For them the gracious Duncan have I murdered.

    Comment on these lines.

12. At the beginning of Act III before the Macbeths' banquet, Macbeth turns to Banquo and comments "Here's our chief guest" when he knows that his friend will be murdered before the feast begins. Macbeth's words are an example of _____. (Fill in the blank.)

13. Read this line spoken by one of the witches: "Fair is foul, and foul is fair."
    This line is an example of _____ (Fill in the blank.)

14 - 19:
    (a) Identify the SPEAKER and
    (b) Explain the SIGNIFICANCE of the following passages:

14. The Thane of Cawdor lives: why do you dress me
    In borrowed robes?

15. For brave _____ well he deserves that name—
    Disdaining fortune, with his brandished steel,
    Which smoked with — execution,
    Like valor's minion carved out his passage
    Till he faced the slave;
    Which nev'r shook hands, nor bade farewell to him,
    Till he unseamed him from the nave to th' chops,
    And fixed his head upon our battlements.

16. But 'tis strange;
    And oftentimes, to win us to our harm,
    The instruments of darkness tell us truths,
    Win us with honest trifles, to betray's [betray us]
    In deepest consequence.

17. He was a gentleman on whom I built
    An absolute trust.

18. Will all great Neptune's ocean wash this blood
    Clean from my hand?

19. This murderous shaft that's shot
    Hath not yet lighted [reached its target], and our safest way
    Is to avoid the aim.

20. Identify the function of the first scene of the play and explain how it contributes to
    the main theme.

21. Banquo is highly respected and loved throughout Scotland. Explain how Macbeth persuades despicable thugs to kill this noble thane.

22. What pretext does Macbeth give Macduff and others present for killing Duncan's servants? What is the real reason for his killing them?

23. If you were the producer of this play, how would you stage the entrance of Duncan's ghost that appears during the Macbeths' banquet? Where would you place Macbeth's seat at the banquet table?

Macbeth Acts IV–V Test

Name _____

1. At the beginning of Act IV, when Macbeth returns to the witches to get their help, they show him four apparitions. With reference to at least three of the apparitions, explain what they symbolize.

2. Why do the murders of Lady Macduff and her son emphasize Macbeth's descent into utter villainy?

3. Some producers of this play cut out the scene that shows the murders of Lady Macduff and her child. What is your reaction to this decision?

4. Give some reasons for the scene between Malcolm and Macduff during which Malcolm feigns a corrupt nature.

5. Perhaps the most memorable lines in the play are these:
   Tomorrow and tomorrow and tomorrow
   Creeps in this petty pace from day to day,
   To the last syllable of recorded time
   And all our yesterdays have lighted fools
   The way to dusty death. Out, out, brief candle!
   Life's but a walking shadow, a poor player
   That struts and frets his hour upon the stage
   And then is heard no more. It is a tale
   Told by an idiot, full of sound and fury,
   Signifying nothing.

   Give the context then, in your own words, summarize the main idea conveyed in this passage. Then state and defend your opinion of Macbeth at this point in the play.

6. What is the fate of Lady Macbeth?

7. Summarize the tremendous changes that take place in the relationship between Macbeth and his wife throughout the course of the play.

8. Why does Shakespeare give the closing lines to Malcolm?

9. We talked about the Elizabethan worldview. Provide one example of the way this play reflects the mindset of Shakespeare's contemporaries.

10. The atmosphere of *Macbeth* contributes significantly to its meaning. Identify the play's dominant mood and briefly comment on it.

11. List two instances that reinforce the appearance versus reality theme in the last two Acts.

12. Comment on the language of this play: What is Shakespeare's dominant poetic mode? When and why does he vary this language?

13 - 16. Comment on the significance of these four passages:

Something wicked this way comes.

There are a crew of wretched souls
That stay [wait for] his cure; their malady convinces [defies]
The great assay of art [medical efforts]; but at his touch,

Such sanctity hath heaven given his hand,
They presently amend [immediately recover].

All the perfumes of Arabia will not sweeten this little hand.

They have tied me to a stake; I cannot fly,
But bearlike I must fight the course. What's he
That was not born of woman? Such a one
Am I to fear, or none.

17. *Macbeth* was written, in part, to flatter James I. Give several examples from the play that illustrate how Shakespeare achieves this tribute to his patron.

18. Give your opinion about the extent to which Macbeth is a tragic hero in the Aristotelian sense.

19. What is your reaction to Shakespeare's tragic hero?

17th century Poetry Test

Name _____

The poetry you will need to respond to these questions is attached to the back of the test.

1. Define the following terms: paradox; metaphysical conceit.

2. What poetic device is Donne using here: "Batter my heart, three-personed God"?

3. Explain Donne's metaphoric language in the following lines:
   > for you [God]
   > As yet but knock, breathe, shine and seek to mend;
   > . . . and bend
   > Your force to break, blow, burn and make me new.

4. Read these lines from Donne's poem "Valediction Forbidding Mourning" and explain their meaning:
   > But we by a love so much refined,
   > That ourselves know not what it is,
   > Inter-assurèd of the mind,
   > Care less eyes, lips, and hands to miss.

5. List several differences in the styles of Donne and Herbert's poetry.

6. Refer to Herbert's poem "Virtue." What idea is central to this poem?

7. Refer to "Easter Wings." What is Herbert mainly concerned about in this poem?

8. One of Herbert's poems is entitled "The Altar." Why does Herbert state that his altar is broken?

9. Herbert's poem "Love 3" is a dialogue. Who are the two speakers?

10. As concisely as possible, define Andrew Marvell's three-part argument in his poem entitled "To His Coy Mistress."

11. Refer to Ben Jonson's poem that mourns his little son's death. Summarize the main ideas the poet expresses.

12. Refer to Suckling's poem "Out upon it, I have loved." It becomes immediately apparent that Suckling's speaker adopts a highly ironic attitude to love although the poem is a compliment to the woman he loves. Explain this apparent contradiction.

13. Another of Suckling's poems begins with this line: "Why so pale and wan, fond lover?" What advice does the speaker give the "fond lover"?

14. A famous poem by Richard Lovelace is entitled "To Lucasta, on Going to the Wars." What assurance does the speaker wish to impress upon the lady he loves?

15. Like most great epics, Milton's *Paradise Lost* begins with an extended _____. (Fill in the blank.)

16. What is Satan's tone throughout the section of *Paradise Lost* that we read?

17. Having been thrown out of heaven, Satan confers with Beelzebub. What is Beelzebub's response to Satan's plan to strike out again at Almighty God?

18. Why do you think some poets such as William Blake insisted that Satan not God is the hero of Milton's epic?

"Elegy Written in a Country Churchyard" Test

Name _____

1. What dominant mood is established in the opening stanzas?

2. What is Gray's opinion of the rural peasants who lie in their graves around him? Why is this attitude typically romantic?

3. What is Gray's opinion of England's upper class?

4. What is the poet's main concern throughout the Elegy?

5. Summarize the meaning of this stanza:
   Full many a gem of purest ray serene
   The dark unfathomed caves of ocean bear:
   Full many a flower is born to blush unseen,
   And waste its sweetness on the desert air.

6. The poet mentions Oliver Cromwell and other famous men who significantly impacted English life. Give the name of at least one of these other men.

7. Briefly state Gray's opinion of John Hampden.

8. Read these lines:

> Let not Ambition mock their useful toil,
>
> Their homely joys and destiny obscure;
>
> Nor Grandeur hear with a disdainful smile
>
> The short and simple annals of the poor.

To what or whom does the poet refer with the words "Ambition" and "Grandeur"? Explain the poet's use of the word "annals."

9. Read these lines:

> Can storied urn or animated bust
>
> Back to its mansion call the fleeting breath?

What is meant by a "storied urn"? an "animated bust"?

10. What does Gray suggest is greatly desired by all men including the humble poor of his village?

11. What does the poet suggest will happen to him at the end of the poem? Be as specific as possible.

12. Gray is a transitional writer. Mention some traits in his Elegy that represent both the eighteenth-century neoclassic style and romantic preoccupations.

13. Write out a one-sentence theme for this great poem.

Romantic Poetry Test

Name _____

1 - 5: Identify the poet and poem from which the following lines are taken and make some significant observations about the lines; for example, you could discuss the context, the way the lines reflect romantic ideals, or you could comment on pertinent poetic devices. Be precise and specific.

1. Great God! I'd rather be
A pagan suckled in a creed outworn;
So might I, standing on this pleasant lea [meadow],
Have glimpses that would make me less forlorn...

Poet:

Comments:

2. Never did sun more beautifully steep
In his first splendor, valley, rock, or hill;
Ne'er saw I, never felt, a calm so deep!
The river glideth at his own sweet will...

Poet:

Comments:

3. When I behold, upon the night's starred face,
Huge cloudy symbols of a high romance,
And think that I may never live to trace
Their shadows with the magic hand of chance. . .

Poet:

Comments:

4.   Down dropped the breeze, the sails dropped down,
'Twas sad as sad could be;
And we did speak only to break
The silence of the sea…
Day after day, day after day,
We stuck, no breath nor motion;
As idle as a painted ship
Upon a painted ocean.

Poet:

Comments:

5.   …would I were steadfast as thou art—
Not in lone splendor hung aloft the night—
And watching with eternal lids apart,
Like nature's patient, sleepless Eremite [hermit],
The moving waters at their priestlike task
Of pure ablution round earth's human shores…

Poet:

Comments:

6.   Who was the Ozymandias of Shelley's sonnet?

7.   Define a Byronic hero.

8.   Why is "Kubla Khan" a fragment?

9. Briefly explain why it is possible to read "The Rime of the Ancient Mariner" as an allegory of crime, punishment, and forgiveness.

10. Identify the various types of imagery in Keats's ode "To Autumn." What is another organizational device that the poet uses in this poem?

11. What makes Keats's ode a characteristically romantic poem?

Victorian Poetry Test

Name _____

The poetry you will need to respond to these questions is attached to the back of the test.

1. Explain why Browning's celebrated poem "My Last Duchess" is a dramatic monologue.

2. Refer to the poem and explain why the duke believes himself to be reasonable and humble although the reader understands the reverse to be the case.

3. Refer to Tennyson's "Ulysses." Explain why this poem explores, in part, intellectual striving.

4. Based on "Ulysses," what is Tennyson's attitude to growing old? How does his attitude differ from our contemporary attitudes to aging?

5. Refer to Section 54 of Tennyson's elegy *In Memoriam*. What do these lines convey about Tennyson's religious faith?

6. Critics contend that Tennyson's theme in "The Lady of Shalott" involves the plight of the artist, that the artist is destined to be alone in order to pursue his or her art. Based on the poem, briefly defend this reading.

7. Refer to Housman's poem "To an Athlete Dying Young." Summarize the events and ideas found in this poem.

8. Refer to the poem entitled "With Rue My Heart Is Laden." What is its theme? Explain the references to brooks "too broad for leaping" and roses fading.

9. Why is the title of Hopkins's poem "God's Grandeur" appropriate?

10. Refer to Hardy's "Channel Firing." What is the dominant tone? What is the perspective?

11. Hardy concludes this poem with several allusions. Identify the allusions. What do they imply?

12. Refer to "When I Was One-and-Twenty" by A. E. Housman. Briefly state your personal reaction to this poem.

13. Refer to "Up-Hill." Identify the speakers. What is the tone of the first speaker's questions? What is the tone of the second speaker's replies?

14. Refer to Hardy's poem about the *Titanic*'s fate. Why does Hardy imply that the ship's fate is ironic?

15. Hardy's poem is divided into two halves. What is the subject of each half? What does the poet conclude about the ultimate reason for the tragedy?

Modern Poetry Test

Name _____

The poetry you will need to respond to these questions is attached to the back of the test.

1. Refer to Dylan Thomas's poem "Do Not Go Gentle into That Good Night." What is the poet's concern? Explain how he uses three types of men to expand on his argument.

2. Many other poets have explored the same theme as Thomas. How is Thomas's poem different from the treatment of the same idea by two <u>Victorian</u> poets?

3. Think about "Church Going" by Philip Larkin. What is the dominant tone of the poem? Who is the speaker? How involved is the speaker as he inspects the church building?

4. Refer to "Musée des Beaux Arts" by W. H. Auden. Define Auden's theme and with detailed reference to at least two of Brueghel's paintings, discuss how the poet conveys this main idea.

5. Think about the excerpt we read from "The Hollow Men" by T. S. Eliot. How does the poet depict modern men in these stanzas?

6. Think about "Base Details" by Siegfried Sassoon. How does this poem convey the poet's hatred of war?

7. Refer to "Anthem for Doomed Youth" by Wilfred Owen. Identify the various contrasts the poet makes between the two halves of this sonnet.

8. What poetic device does Owen use in the first line of each half of the sonnet?

9. Explain the reference in the last line of Owen's poem.

10. Explain how the theme of nostalgia is explored in two modern poems we have read.

11. Refer to "Aubade" by Philip Larkin. What central idea does the poet explore in this poem? Discuss how Larkin conveys his theme.

12. Think about "Digging" by Seamus Heaney. How does the hard labor of digging pervade the poem?

13. How does Heaney relate the toil of digging to his own work?

14. Refer to "The Love Song of J. Alfred Prufrock." With reference to several sections of the poem, explain how those sections convey a grim picture of Prufrock's self-consciousness.

Printed in the United States
By Bookmasters